FROM DAY ONE

FROM DAY ONE

THRIVING AFTER SALVATION

ANGEL ADAMS

Foreword by
ADALIS SHUTTLESWORTH
Edited by
LINDA CRABTREE

Without limiting the rights under copyright(s) reserved below, no part of this publication may be reproduced, stored in or introduced into a retrieval system, or transmitted, in any form, or by any means (electronic, mechanical, photocopying, recording, or otherwise) without the prior permission of the publisher and the copyright owner.

The content of this book is provided "AS IS." The Publisher and the Author make no guarantees or warranties as to the accuracy, adequacy or completeness of or results to be obtained from using the content of this book, including any information that can be accessed through hyperlinks or otherwise, and expressly disclaim any warranty expressed or implied, including but not limited to implied warranties of merchantability or fitness for a particular purpose. This limitation of liability shall apply to any claim or cause whatsoever whether such claim or cause arises in contract, tort, or otherwise. In short, you, the reader, are responsible for your choices and the results they bring.

The scanning, uploading, and distributing of this book via the internet or via any other means without the permission of the publisher and copyright owner is illegal and punishable by law. Please purchase only authorized copies, and do not participate in or encourage piracy of copyrighted materials. Your support of the author's rights is appreciated.

Scripture quotations marked (NIV) are taken from the Holy Bible, New International Version®, NIV®. Copyright © 1973, 1978, 1984, 2011 by Biblica, Inc.™ Used by permission of Zondervan. All rights reserved worldwide. www.zondervan.com The "NIV" and "New International Version" are trademarks registered in the United States Patent and Trademark Office by Biblica, Inc.™

Scripture quotations marked (NLT) are taken from the *Holy Bible*, New Living Translation, copyright ©1996, 2004, 2015 by Tyndale House Foundation. Used by permission of Tyndale House Publishers, Carol Stream, Illinois 60188. All rights reserved.

Scripture marked (NKJV) is taken from the New King James Version®. Copyright © 1982 by Thomas Nelson. Used by permission. All rights reserved.

Scripture quotations marked (AMPC) are taken from the Amplified® Bible (AMPC), Copyright © 1954, 1958, 1962, 1964, 1965, 1987 by The Lockman Foundation. Used by permission. lockman.org

Copyright © 2023 by Angela Adams. All rights reserved.

Book design by eBook Prep
www.ebookprep.com

February 2023
ISBN: 978-1-64457-607-6

Rise UP Publications
644 Shrewsbury Commons Ave
Ste 249
Shrewsbury PA 17361
United States of America
www.riseUPpublications.com
Phone: 866-846-5123

This book is dedicated to my husband, Scotty, and my sweet babies, Abbey, Mac, and Ben. I am so thankful for you. You support me and make me laugh every day. Scotty, you have changed my life by loving me like Christ loves His Church. You are the greatest gift I will ever receive outside of salvation. Abbey, your life is an answer to prayer. We prayed for a child, and God gave us the best in you. Mac, you are a sign that God always gives us more than we ask. Ben, you are the miracle surprise who showed us God has a great sense of humor. Thank you all for being my people. I love you.

FOREWORD

This book is exactly what you need if you are in ministry. As an evangelist's wife of 16 years and a minister myself, I have seen a growing trend in the oversimplification of becoming a born-again, spirit-filled believer. Don't get me wrong, the process is easy since Jesus Christ did all the work for us but like any covenant, we must do our part to see the benefits!

The prayer of salvation is the most critical decision someone will ever make. It's a tremendous experience that brings a person from death to life. What happens afterward? Do we give people a giant hug and wish them well in life? Do we hand them a book and hope we meet them in the air on the day of judgment? There is another step the believer must take. And I believe this book will help!

The day my daughter was born was the best day of my life. I held her in my arms and wrapped her in a soft pink blanket, I had never realized how much love you can have for someone you just met! But if that was the end of the journey for my daughter and me, our world today would be dramatically different. Think about it, if I had placed my daughter in the

FOREWORD

warm bassinet, wished her good luck and grabbed my keys, and went home, what would have happened? I would most likely get put into a 5150 psychiatric hold.

From Day One is a step-by-step guide to what new believers should do for the first 12 days after salvation. This book is practical and hands-on while at the same time connecting some of the dots that are required to make lasting changes in a new Christian's life. From the importance of water baptism to a believer's God-given authority and everything in between.

Pastor Angel's love for humanity and concern for the body of Christ exudes through the pages of this book. Paired with the mighty Word of God, you can rest assured that each new believer in your life will have the help he or she needs to live the victorious life God created them to have!

Adalis Shuttlesworth, Pastor

INTRODUCTION

I'm writing this book to help brand-new Christians get a running start to a life of power and purpose. You don't have to waste one second. You are now part of an ever-increasing kingdom.

Some people say their moment of salvation was the high point of their lives, but I'm here to tell you that your moment of salvation was just the start. You'll only go up from here. God has set you on a path of ever-increasing faith.

I'm also writing this book to help those who have served Christ for a longer period but feel dull and powerless in their walk. You may be wondering, "Is this all there is?". There is more! There is an abundant life waiting for you. But you will not enter it passively; you will have to take it by force.

Wherever you are in your walk with God today, be encouraged—there is a higher place. You'll never reach the end of what God has for you on this earth. And the journey to Heaven is meant to be filled with peace, joy, and power!

PART I

GETTING STARTED

1

WHAT JUST HAPPENED TO ME?

Welcome to the Family of God! Since you're reading this, I assume you have prayed to receive Jesus Christ as your Lord and Savior. It's the best decision you'll ever make. Committing your whole life to cultivating this relationship with your Savior from DAY ONE will put you on a path to an overcoming life.

Maybe you got saved in a church service where you walked up to an altar to pray. Maybe you prayed to receive salvation in the privacy of your own home, or perhaps your friend led you to Jesus. Regardless of your physical location, something happened in the spiritual world that has changed things for you forever.

> For he has rescued us from the dominion of darkness and brought us into the kingdom of the Son he loves, in whom we have redemption, the forgiveness of sins.
>
> — COLOSSIANS 1:13-14 NIV

YOU LIVE IN A NEW KINGDOM

You are no longer under the power of darkness, sin, sickness, and death. God has taken you out of the hands of your enemy, Satan, and put you into the kingdom of His Son. In the Spirit, your address has changed from Dead Drive to Alive Avenue. You can't see it, but it's more real than what you can see. What a reason to celebrate! Even the angels are rejoicing today because you got saved.

> In the same way, I tell you, there is rejoicing in the presence of the angels of God over one sinner who repents.
>
> — LUKE 15:10 NIV

Satan has no right to control you anymore. You don't belong to him. He'll try to control you, but His reign is over if you decide never to return to your old life. He's no match for God, and God is your Father now. Our Father takes His family very seriously. If someone messes with you, they're messing with Him. All of God's favor and power are behind you. You are SAVED!

> —for whoever touches you touches the apple of his (God's) eye—
>
> — ZECHARIAH 2:8 NIV

YOU ARE A NEW CREATION

This "you" has never existed before. You may look and feel the same, but you are new. Everything from your past is forgiven. The slate is wiped clean. But, it is more profound than forgiveness. You are born-again, just like Jesus explained to Nicodemus in John 3:3-8.

> Jesus replied, "I tell you the truth, unless you are born again, you cannot see the Kingdom of God." "What do you mean?" exclaimed Nicodemus. "How can an old man go back into his mother's womb and be born again?" Jesus replied, "I assure you, no one can enter the Kingdom of God without being born of water and the Spirit. Humans can reproduce only human life, but the Holy Spirit gives birth to spiritual life. So don't be surprised when I say, 'You must be born again.' The wind blows wherever it wants. Just as you can hear the wind but can't tell where it comes from or where it is going, so you can't explain how people are born of the Spirit."
>
> — JOHN 3:3-8 NLT

Peter describes it like this:

> For you have been born again, but not to a life that will quickly end. Your new life will last forever because it comes from the eternal, living word of God.
>
> — 1 PETER 1:23 NLT

It is as if your life is starting over in God's eyes. Yesterday, you were a sinner bound for Hell; today, you are a saint bound for Heaven and a partaker of every single promise God made to His children. Don't let anyone convince you otherwise.

Believing you are a new creation is crucial to experiencing all the good things God has in store for you. You might be tempted to feel guilt and shame over the life you used to live, but that life is over. This is how the apostle Paul describes it:

> Therefore, if anyone is in Christ, he is a new creation; old things have passed away; behold, all things have become new.
>
> — II CORINTHIANS 5:17 NKJV

> My old self has been crucified with Christ. It is no longer I who live, but Christ lives in me. So I live in this earthly body by trusting in the Son of God, who loved me and gave himself for me.
>
> — GALATIANS 2:20 NLT

At the time I am writing this book, I have been a Christian for 28 years. Until ten years ago, I didn't understand who I was in Christ. As a result, I was tormented by guilt and shame over my past life. Once I got that revelation, I've never been the same. It's not just a new level; it's a new galaxy!

You are now "in Christ" and a recipient of every promise in the Word.

Go through your Bible and underline every place you see "in Christ," "in Him," "by Christ," "through Christ," or "with Christ." This opens your eyes to who you are now and what belongs to you. For example…

> God made him who had no sin to be sin for us,
> so that **in him** we might become the
> righteousness of God.
>
> — 2 CORINTHIANS 5:21 NIV

This exercise is a great first Bible study for you. Spend some time each day searching for these Scriptures. Most importantly, when you read them, believe them.

Read out loud, "God made him who had no sin to be sin for us, so that in him we might become the righteousness of God." Then say, "In Jesus, I have become the righteousness of God." Then say it again and again. Begin to thank God out loud, "Thank you, God, that in Jesus I am the righteousness of God!"

Do this with each of the scriptures you find, and you will understand who you are in Christ. There are literally hundreds of these scriptures to dig through. It is like a treasure hunt for a prize worth much more than gold or silver.

EVERY CURSE IS BROKEN

According to Strong's Concordance, a curse is what has "to go down" (penalties received) due to condemnation. Before you were saved, you were under condemnation because of your sin. Now, you have been released from condemnation and set up for the blessings of God. The difference between the blessing and the curse is illustrated in Deuteronomy 28. Verses 1-14 describe the blessings of obeying the voice of God and His commandments.

> If you fully obey the Lord your God and carefully keep all his commands that I am giving you today, the Lord your God will set you high above all the nations of the world. You will experience all these blessings if you obey the Lord your God: Your towns and your fields will be blessed. Your children and your crops will be blessed. The offspring of your herds and flocks will be blessed. Your fruit baskets and breadboards will be blessed. Wherever you go and whatever you do, you will be blessed. The Lord will conquer your enemies when they attack you. They will attack you from one direction, but they will scatter from you in seven! The Lord will guarantee a blessing on everything you do and will fill your storehouses with grain. The Lord your God will bless you in the land he is giving you. If you obey the commands of the Lord your God and walk in his ways, the Lord will establish you as his holy people as he swore he would do. Then all the nations of the world will see that you are a people claimed by the Lord, and they will stand in awe of you. The Lord will give you prosperity in the land he swore to your ancestors to give you, blessing you with many children,

> numerous livestock, and abundant crops.
> The Lord will send rain at the proper time
> from his rich treasury in the heavens and
> will bless all the work you do. You will
> lend to many nations, but you will never
> need to borrow from them. If you listen to
> these commands of the Lord your God that
> I am giving you today, and if you carefully
> obey them, the Lord will make you the
> head and not the tail, and you will always
> be on top and never at the bottom. You
> must not turn away from any of the
> commands I am giving you today, nor
> follow after other gods and worship them.
>
> — DEUTERONOMY 28:1-14 NLT

Verses 15-68 of Deuteronomy 28 describe the curses for disobeying God's commandments.

> But if you refuse to listen to the Lord your
> God and do not obey all the commands
> and decrees I am giving you today, all
> these curses will come and overwhelm
> you: Your towns and your fields will be
> cursed. Your fruit baskets and breadboards
> will be cursed. Your children and your
> crops will be cursed. The offspring of your
> herds and flocks will be cursed. Wherever
> you go and whatever you do, you will be
> cursed. The Lord himself will send on you
> curses, confusion, and frustration in
> everything you do, until at last you are

> completely destroyed for doing evil and abandoning me. The Lord will afflict you with diseases until none of you are left in the land you are about to enter and occupy. The Lord will strike you with wasting diseases, fever, and inflammation, with scorching heat and drought, and with blight and mildew. These disasters will pursue you until you die. The skies above will be as unyielding as bronze, and the earth beneath will be as hard as iron. The Lord will change the rain that falls on your land into powder, and dust will pour down from the sky until you are destroyed. The Lord will cause you to be defeated by your enemies. You will attack your enemies from one direction, but you will scatter from them in seven! You will be an object of horror to all the kingdoms of the earth.
>
> — DEUTERONOMY 28:15-25 NLT

The curse of the law consists primarily of spiritual death, sickness, and poverty. You are now free from all these things! As you grow in your knowledge of the Word of God, this becomes more and more real to you.

> But Christ has rescued us from the curse pronounced by the law. When he was hung on the cross, he took upon himself the curse for our wrongdoing. For it is written in the Scriptures, "Cursed is everyone who is hung on a tree." Through Christ Jesus,

> God has blessed the Gentiles with the same blessing he promised to Abraham, so that we who are believers might receive the promised Holy Spirit through faith.
>
> — GALATIANS 3:13-14 NLT

What does Paul mean when he declares, "Christ has rescued us from the curse"? He means the power of the things that used to harass you is broken. If you struggle with alcohol addiction, its power is broken. If you struggle with anger, it is broken. If you've lived in fear all your life, you don't have to fear for another day. If everyone in your family got cancer, you don't have to get it. If your family has been in debt and poverty for generations, you will be the first to come out of it. Your past is no longer a predictor of your future. It doesn't matter what destructive pattern has run your life in the past. You are now free because of the sacrifice of Jesus.

But, wait…there's more! Galatians 3:14 says God has blessed the Gentiles with the same blessing he promised to Abraham. Not only is the curse broken, but you have become a recipient of every promised blessing in the Bible.

If I had to pick a favorite Scripture, this would be it.

> For no matter how many promises God has made, they are "Yes" in Christ. And so through him the "Amen" is spoken by us to the glory of God.
>
> — 2 CORINTHIANS 1:20 NIV

Every. Single. Promise. There are thousands of promises in God's Word. If you are "In Christ," God's answer to every one of them is YES! Your job is to say, "Amen," which means so be it.

We could spend the rest of our lives rejoicing over this one Scripture. Oh, how wonderful our Father is to us, His children!

ADDITIONAL RESOURCES

- *In Him* by Kenneth E. Hagin
- *Redeemed from Poverty, Sickness, and Spiritual Death* by Kenneth E. Hagin

2

NEXT STEPS

SEEKING AND WORKING

The trajectory of your new life in Christ is determined by what you do next. If you do nothing, over time, you will find yourself back where you started before you got saved. If you give your time, passion, and energy to growing in the Lord, amazing confidence and power will be yours.

> Dear friends, you always followed my instructions when I was with you. And now that I am away, it is even more important. Work hard to show the results of your salvation, obeying God with deep reverence and fear. For God is working in you, giving you the desire and the power to do what pleases him.
>
> — PHILIPPIANS 2:12-13 NLT

Paul tells us to "work hard" to show the results of our salvation. Then he encourages us—God is giving us "the desire and the power" to do it. You and God are working together to see everything that Jesus died to give you become a reality in your life.

Some people miss it here because they think God automatically makes everything that He wants for them come to pass. God doesn't work this way. For instance, Jesus gave His life so we could be saved, but we have a part to fulfill in receiving salvation; it is not given to us automatically. The path to salvation is systematically laid out in the Bible. We must either seek it out ourselves or hear someone preach it to us before receiving it. Then we must take the steps to receive it. (Believe and Confess)

> Because if you acknowledge and confess with your lips that Jesus is Lord and in your heart believe (adhere to, trust in, and rely on the truth) that God raised Him from the dead, you will be saved. For with the heart a person believes (adheres to, trusts in, and relies on Christ) and so is justified (declared righteous, acceptable to God), and with the mouth he confesses (declares openly and speaks out freely his faith) and confirms [his] salvation.
>
> — ROMANS 10:9-10 AMPC

It is the same with living a victorious, fearless, joyful Christian life. You must find the truth in the Word of God and follow the path the Word lays out. You must practice things like devouring the Word, believing the Word, obeying the Word, and developing spiritual disciplines.

> "And from the days of John the Baptist until the present time, the kingdom of heaven has endured violent assault, and violent men seize it by force [as a precious prize—a share in the heavenly kingdom is sought with most ardent zeal and intense exertion]."
>
> — MATTHEW 11:12 AMPC

The key to an upward trajectory in God's Kingdom is to seek Him like a precious prize, with ardent zeal and intense exertion. We are the "violent men" Jesus is speaking of in Matthew 11:12. We are not to be physically violent. One definition of the word violent in this verse is "fired up." We must be fired up about the things of God. Seeking God is not a hobby or some side thing in our lives. It is our reason for living! We are part of an ever-increasing kingdom. You can go continuously up from here by devoting yourself to violently seizing everything in God's Kingdom.

I've loved the Lord since the day I got saved. I have never considered myself complacent about the things of God. I got saved in 1994 and experienced a modicum of growth over the years. However, in 2017, I realized what Matthew 11:12 meant about being violent in possessing the things of God. I got connected with the right teachers and ministries. I heard and saw the Word preached in power. I committed myself to getting all I could. And, God worked with me as Philippians 2:13 says. The growth I've seen in my life since cannot be compared to the first 23 years of being saved. Nothing is the same! A violent increase has begun in my life and it will never stop. Praise God!

Don't waste any time. If you are a brand-new Christian, you can skip all those years of little growth and launch into a life of maturity and power. If you've been saved for years, let this be your tipping point. Decide today that you are going to get serious about the things of God and get violent about possessing everything He has for you. It's not too early and it's not too late.

These next chapters contain the necessary components for a victorious life. They do not occur in order of importance because they are all important. You do not have to check one thing off this list before implementing another. Do them all and do them with passion.

> **Note:** At the end of each chapter, I include a list of books for additional reading. This is part of being one of the "violent" who takes the things of God by force. Don't settle for a little knowledge. Dig deeper. Keep learning.

I suggest each specific book because who you listen to matters. If you trace the roots of powerful Christian men and women, you will find common threads; they have been under the same people or teachings. You cannot pick up just any book in the Religion section of Barnes and Noble or Amazon. Get connected to the giants in the faith by reading their books and watching their sermons. Get connected in person to whoever is ministering in power today! Dr. Rodney Howard-Browne, Ted Shuttlesworth Sr., Jesse Duplantis, and Jonathan Shuttlesworth are just a few who minister today. You can visit their meetings in person. Whatever you must invest to do this, it's worth it.

ADDITIONAL RESOURCES

- *When You See the Invisible You Can Do the Impossible* by Oral Roberts
- *How to Dominate in a Wicked Nation* by Jonathan Shuttlesworth

PART II

ENSURING SUCCESS

3

BAPTISM

BAPTIZED IN WATER

Water baptism is often a new believer's first outward act of obedience. It is commanded by Jesus, himself.

> Jesus came and told his disciples, "I have been given all authority in heaven and on earth. Therefore, go and make disciples of all the nations, baptizing them in the name of the Father and the Son and the Holy Spirit."
>
> — MATTHEW 28:18-19 NLT

Jesus also modeled water baptism for us. Although he did not have to repent of any sin, he was baptized to be an example for us. We should not take this lightly. We should do all that God commands because we want to please him and because there is a blessing attached to obedience.

> Then Jesus went from Galilee to the Jordan River to be baptized by John. But John tried to talk him out of it. "I am the one who needs to be baptized by you," he said, "so why are you coming to me?" But Jesus said, "It should be done, for we must carry out all that God requires." So John agreed to baptize him.
>
> — MATTHEW 3:13-15 NLT

Water baptism is an outward sign of an inward work that happens at salvation. When you got saved, something wonderful happened inside of you. You were made new! But people can't see the inward change with their eyes. Baptism is a tangible thing people can see. You're giving testimony of something Jesus has done on the inside of you. It symbolizes that you have died, been buried, and resurrected to a brand-new life with Jesus Christ. Praise God!

Your friends and family can't feel what you felt at salvation. They can't know what happened in your mind or your heart. But they can see you are publicly declaring to the world that you are a new person because of Jesus Christ. Your baptism is a perfect chance to invite your family and friends to know the new you. Through your obedience, some of them can be saved. Every command of God has a purpose and a blessing attached to it.

Water baptism doesn't save you; it declares you are saved. It won't do an unsaved person any good to get baptized. It will only make them wet—not clean. Peter says water baptism isn't the removal of dirt but the pledge of a clear conscience toward God. You don't do it to save yourself; you do it because Jesus saved you.

> ...and this water symbolizes baptism that now saves you also—not the removal of dirt from the body but the pledge of a clear conscience toward God. It saves you by the resurrection of Jesus Christ,
>
> — 1 PETER 3:21 NIV

THE IMPORTANCE OF BAPTISM

Every born-again believer who has confessed Jesus Christ as Lord and Savior should be baptized in water. In Acts 2, the believers are born-again and baptized on the Day of Pentecost.

> Those who accepted his message were baptized, and about three thousand were added to their number that day.
>
> — ACTS 2:41 NIV

In Acts 8, Philip leads the Ethiopian eunuch to salvation and he is baptized.

> Now as they went down the road, they came to some water. And the eunuch said, "See, here is water. What hinders me from being baptized?" Then Philip said, "If you believe with all your heart, you may." And

> he answered and said, "I believe that Jesus Christ is the Son of God." So he commanded the chariot to stand still. And both Philip and the eunuch went down into the water, and he baptized him.
>
> — ACTS 8:36-38 NKJV

Infants who can't decide to follow Jesus should be dedicated to the Lord by their parents. Baby dedication is a promise made by parents to raise their children to know Jesus. It also links the child to a church family who should promise to help him or her know the Lord and receive salvation when they're older.

THE METHOD OF BAPTISM

Believers should be baptized by immersion. Immersion means being fully "dunked" underwater. This is the example we see in scripture. Always follow the example you see in the Word. This is something to remember in all things. Church traditions are not always in line with the Word. If a tradition is not written in Scripture, it has no value. Scripture doesn't mention anyone being "sprinkled" with water for baptism.

When Jesus was baptized, Mark 1:10 says, "As Jesus was coming up out of the water…". He was fully in the water. When the eunuch was baptized, Acts 8:38 says, "And both Philip and the eunuch went down into the water…"

This is significant because water baptism tells the world you have died to your old nature (or old self) and been buried (going under the water) and you have been raised to new life in Christ (coming up out of the water). Dr. Rodney Howard-

Browne says, "When something dies, you dig a hole, and you bury it. You don't sprinkle dirt on its head!" The old man is dead, and we are raised to new life. Go under to show the world what Jesus did for you.

When new believers are baptized at New Day Christian Center, the whole congregation sings "I Have Decided to Follow Jesus." This song is a powerful statement. You can sing it now as a declaration; you are never turning back!

> I have decided to follow Jesus;
> I have decided to follow Jesus;
> I have decided to follow Jesus;
> No turning back, no turning back.
>
> Tho' none go with me, I still will follow,
> Tho' none go with me, I still will follow,
> Tho' none go with me, I still will follow;
> No turning back, no turning back.
>
> The world behind me, the cross before me,
> The world behind me, the cross before me;
> The world behind me, the cross before me;
> No turning back, no turning back.
>
> Will you decide now to follow Jesus;
> Will you decide now to follow Jesus;
> Will you decide now to follow Jesus;
> No turning back, no turning back.

If you haven't been baptized in water, ask your pastor or a church leader today—don't wait.

ADDITIONAL RESOURCE

- *Run To the Water* by Dr. Rodney Howard-Browne mp3 download

4

HOLY SPIRIT BAPTISM

THE POWER IS YOURS

You need power to live in this world, and the power you need is available. It is the same power Jesus poured out on the Day of Pentecost in Acts 2. It is the power of the Baptism of the Holy Spirit. Your human willpower and passion can only carry you so far; you need supernatural power to live this Christian life victoriously.

When Jesus was speaking to His disciples about His impending death and resurrection, He comforted His friends with these words about the Helper He was about to send:

> "But now I go away to Him who sent Me, and none of you asks Me, 'Where are You going?' But because I have said these things to you, sorrow has filled your heart. Nevertheless I tell you the truth. It is to your advantage that I go away; for if I do not go away, the Helper will not come to

> you; but if I depart, I will send Him to you."
>
> — JOHN 16:5-7 NKJV

Jesus Himself said He was sending a Helper so great that it was better for Him to leave. That is hard to fathom! How could anything be better for you than having Jesus around? This Helper is the Holy Spirit, the Spirit of God. Jesus went back to His Father, but He sent the Holy Spirit to us to live IN us. Think about it… When Jesus was on this earth, He could only be in one place at one time. He was in a mortal body. Once He was resurrected and ascended to His Father, He could send the Holy Spirit to live in every believer.

Every believer receives the indwelling presence of the Holy Spirit at salvation. Romans 8:9 says, "…Now if any man does not have the Spirit of Christ, he is not his." However, there is a second work of the Holy Spirit that follows being born-again. It is what Jesus spoke of in Acts 1.

> On one occasion, while he was eating with them, he gave them this command: "Do not leave Jerusalem, but wait for the gift my Father promised, which you have heard me speak about. For John baptized with water, but in a few days you will be baptized with the Holy Spirit.
> But you will receive power when the Holy Spirit comes on you; and you will be my witnesses in Jerusalem, and in all Judea and Samaria, and to the ends of the earth."
>
> — ACTS 1:4-5, 8 NIV

Jesus spoke about the gift of baptism in the Holy Spirit. It was so vital that He instructed the believers not even to try to fulfill the Great Commission until they received it.

The purpose of this baptism is to receive the power to witness and to live. The sign of receiving this baptism is speaking in other tongues.

Acts 2 records the receiving of this promise.

> When the day of Pentecost came, they were all together in one place. Suddenly a sound like the blowing of a violent wind came from heaven and filled the whole house where they were sitting. They saw what seemed to be tongues of fire that separated and came to rest on each of them. All of them were filled with the Holy Spirit and began to speak in other tongues as the Spirit enabled them.
>
> — ACTS 2:1-4 NIV

The people in Jerusalem were so amazed by what was happening to the believers that they asked Peter two questions. "What does this mean?" and "What should we do?" Peter explained that this was the fulfillment of what the prophet Joel had spoken earlier—God was pouring out His Spirit on all flesh! Then, Peter told the people they must repent and be baptized, and they too could receive this promise.

> Peter replied, "Repent and be baptized, every one of you, in the name of Jesus Christ for

> the forgiveness of your sins. And you will receive the gift of the Holy Spirit. The promise is for you and your children and for all who are far off—for all whom the Lord our God will call."
>
> — ACTS 2:38-39 NIV

Three thousand people were born-again on the Day of Pentecost as God poured out His Holy Spirit on the 120 believers. The Holy Spirit Baptism changed everything for them. They moved from fear-filled to faith-filled. They switched from hiding to boldly preaching the gospel wherever they went. Each believer who was baptized began to demonstrate the supernatural power of God through their lives. Receiving this power was the birth of the Church of Jesus Christ which would spread the gospel worldwide. The next chapter of Acts records Peter and John healing the lame man at the Gate Beautiful. This miracle caused well over a thousand more men to be saved. The biblical pattern is that believers were baptized in the Holy Spirit, spoke in tongues, were filled with power, and people were saved. The Baptism of the Holy Spirit took the believers to another level.

According to Peter, this baptism is for you too. He said it is for all whom the Lord our God will call. That means YOU! Receive this Promise today with the same evidence of speaking in other tongues just like these believers.

> The following day he arrived in Caesarea. Cornelius was expecting them and had called together his relatives and close friends. As Peter entered the house,

Cornelius met him and fell at his feet in reverence. But Peter made him get up. "Stand up," he said, "I am only a man myself." While talking with him, Peter went inside and found a large gathering of people. He said to them: "You are well aware that it is against our law for a Jew to associate with or visit a Gentile. But God has shown me that I should not call anyone impure or unclean. So when I was sent for, I came without raising any objection. May I ask why you sent for me?" Cornelius answered: "Three days ago I was in my house praying at this hour, at three in the afternoon. Suddenly a man in shining clothes stood before me and said, 'Cornelius, God has heard your prayer and remembered your gifts to the poor. Send to Joppa for Simon who is called Peter. He is a guest in the home of Simon the tanner, who lives by the sea.' So I sent for you immediately, and it was good of you to come. Now we are all here in the presence of God to listen to everything the Lord has commanded you to tell us." Then Peter began to speak: "I now realize how true it is that God does not show favoritism but accepts from every nation the one who fears him and does what is right. You know the message God sent to the people of Israel, announcing the good news of peace through Jesus Christ, who is Lord of all. You know what has happened throughout the province of Judea, beginning in Galilee after the baptism that John preached— how God anointed Jesus of Nazareth with the Holy Spirit and power, and how he went around doing good and healing all who were under the power of the devil, because God was with him. "We are witnesses of everything he did in the country of the Jews and in Jerusalem. They killed him by hanging him on a cross, but God raised him from the dead on the third day and caused him to be seen. He was not seen by all the people, but by witnesses whom God had already chosen—by us who ate and drank with him after he rose from the dead. He commanded us to preach to the people and to testify that he is the one whom God appointed as judge of the living and the dead. All the prophets testify about him that everyone who believes in him receives forgiveness of sins through his name." While Peter was still speaking these words, the Holy Spirit came on all who heard the message. The circumcised believers who had come with Peter were astonished that the gift of the Holy Spirit had been poured out even on Gentiles. For they heard them speaking in tongues and praising God.

— ACTS 10:24-46 NIV

FROM DAY ONE

> While Apollos was at Corinth, Paul took the road through the interior and arrived at Ephesus. There he found some disciples and asked them, "Did you receive the Holy Spirit when you believed?" They answered, "No, we have not even heard that there is a Holy Spirit." So Paul asked, "Then what baptism did you receive?" "John's baptism," they replied. Paul said, "John's baptism was a baptism of repentance. He told the people to believe in the one coming after him, that is, in Jesus." On hearing this, they were baptized in the name of the Lord Jesus. When Paul placed his hands on them, the Holy Spirit came on them, and they spoke in tongues and prophesied.
>
> — ACTS 19:1-6 NIV

These are just two places where you see believers being baptized in the Holy Spirit and speaking in other tongues. The only thing you must do to receive this promise is to be born-again.

HOW YOU CAN RECEIVE

First, you must believe this baptism is for you. If you are born-again, the baptism is for you. Everything from God is received by faith. If you don't believe it, you won't receive it. Search the scriptures, including the ones I've mentioned here. Read for yourself how the Holy Spirit was poured out on Pentecost, and He is still being poured out today. Acts 2, 8, 9,

10, and 19 show how every believer was baptized in the Holy Spirit.

Follow the pattern in Scripture. The believers only tarried or waited on the baptism in Acts 2. This was because the Holy Spirit was initially poured out on the Day of Pentecost. They began praying and waiting ten days before. In every other instance, the believers received immediately. It is helpful to think of it as if the baptism of the Holy Spirit was a faucet that was opened on the Day of Pentecost. Those first believers were the ones who had to wait. Now, the faucet is running. You only need to get under it and receive it. You do not need to beg for Holy Spirit baptism. Begging would be praying in unbelief. You receive it by faith.

Someone may lay hands on you to receive the Holy Spirit; that is scriptural (Acts 19:6). Expect to receive when someone lays hands on you. You can receive the Holy Spirit on your own in response to hearing the Word that develops your faith. Either way, once you receive the Holy Spirit, He will enable you to speak with other tongues. You will feel a prompting of the Holy Spirit from your gut—not your head, but you must open your mouth and speak as He enables you. He will not speak for you. Once you open your mouth and begin to speak, the heavenly words begin to flow.

Finally, thank the Lord for the supernatural power to witness and to live! Thank Him for the gift of tongues. Now you can pray in tongues every day.

I was baptized in the Holy Spirit in 1995. Because I didn't seek out knowledge on my own or receive much teaching on it, it was over a year before I prayed in tongues again. I was talking to a sister who was a spiritual mentor to me. I told her I hadn't prayed in tongues since I first received the baptism.

She said, "Well, that's easy, honey. You could have been praying in tongues all this time. Just sit down and pray in tongues. You have the ability now!" That's exactly what I did; I've been praying in tongues since that day. You have the precious gift of being able to pray in tongues every day, so do it!

ADDITIONAL READING

- *The Bible Way to Receive the Holy Spirit* by Kenneth E. Hagin
- *The Holy Spirit and His Gifts* by Kenneth E. Hagin
- *The Gifts and Ministries of the Holy Spirit* by Lester Sumrall

5

PRAYER

PRAY DAILY

Most Christians know they should pray, but few know how to pray effectively. There is a way to pray that draws you nearer to God, gets you answers, realizes your heart's desires, and gives you wisdom and power for any situation.

> The earnest (heartfelt, continued) prayer of a righteous man makes tremendous power available [dynamic in its working].
>
> — JAMES 5:16 AMPC

Prayer is a dialogue between you and your Father; you speak, and He speaks. As you pray, you learn to hear God's voice. He reveals His purpose for your life and gives you strategies and plans to make you successful. God is a communicator; He loves to speak to His children. When you pray, you hear Him.

Prayer is also a weapon. As you pray, you get access to tremendous power. There's a saying, "Little prayer, little power. Much prayer, much power."

The Bible gives patterns for prayer. Learn how to pray effectively from the beginning so you won't have to unlearn powerless ways of praying. Following are some prayer keys to help you develop a fruitful prayer life.

PRAY TO THE FATHER IN THE NAME OF JESUS

When teaching His disciples about prayer, Jesus laid out this pattern:

> "At that time you won't need to ask me for anything. I tell you the truth, you will ask the Father directly, and he will grant your request because you use my name. You haven't done this before. Ask, using my name, and you will receive, and you will have abundant joy. Then you will ask in my name. I'm not saying I will ask the Father on your behalf, for the Father himself loves you dearly because you love me and believe that I came from God."
>
> —JOHN 16:23-24, 26-27 NLT

Follow the instructions Jesus gives us on prayer. You cannot go wrong by obeying His words. An effective way to start your prayer is, "Father, I come to you in the Name of Jesus...."

START WITH THANKSGIVING

Complaining repels God's presence. Numbers 11 illustrates how God responds to complaining.

> Now the people complained about their hardships in the hearing of the Lord, and when he heard them his anger was aroused. Then fire from the Lord burned among them and consumed some of the outskirts of the camp. When the people cried out to Moses, he prayed to the Lord and the fire died down. So that place was called Taberah, because fire from the Lord had burned among them.
>
> — NUMBERS 11:1-3 NIV

An atmosphere of complaining and ingratitude makes a comfortable place for demonic presences to thrive; they pull up a chair and make themselves right at home when you complain. That's why complaining never makes you feel better. Praise and thanksgiving attract God. Demons hate to hear God praised. They flee as you speak about the greatness of God and thank Him for everything He has done for you.

> Enter into His gates with thanksgiving, And into His courts with praise. Be thankful to Him, and bless His name.
>
> — PSALMS 100:4 NKJV

Praise takes you into the presence of God. If you don't feel like praising at first, praise Him anyway. If you can't think of anything to praise Him for, praise Him for your breath; praise Him for a sharp mind; praise Him for a beating heart. As you begin to praise, you feel the life of God come into your body, and praise starts flowing before you know it.

My favorite way to praise God is by using His Word. This is the next prayer key.

PRAY THE WORD OF GOD

Learning to pray the Word of God revolutionizes your prayer life. God's Word is His will. Therefore, when you pray what is in his Word, you are praying His will. Talk about effective praying—this is a game-changer! The Bible contains everything God has promised us. Our job is to search the Word to discover and claim those promises. They are for every believer, according to 2 Corinthians 1:20.

> For no matter how many promises God has made, they are "Yes" in Christ. And so through him the "Amen" is spoken by us to the glory of God.
>
> — 2 CORINTHIANS 1:20 NIV

When you pray the Word, you are speaking God's promise back to Him. He is thrilled to honor the Word He spoke; He's the one who came up with it in the first place. In the book of James, James says believers "have not because we ask not" or because "we ask with wrong motives." You're avoiding both things when you pray God's Word; God's Word is His Will!

So, how do you pray God's Word? It's so simple. Since our prayers start with thanksgiving, let's look at a Psalm of praise first. I regularly start my time in prayer with Psalm 103:1-5.

> Bless the Lord, O my soul; And all that is within me, bless His holy name! Bless the Lord, O my soul, And forget not all His benefits: Who forgives all your iniquities, Who heals all your diseases, Who redeems your life from destruction, Who crowns you with lovingkindness and tender mercies, Who satisfies your mouth with good things, So that your youth is renewed like the eagle's.
>
> — PSALMS 103:1-5 NKJV

Make Psalm 103 into a prayer, personalize it, and speak it back to God from your heart. Pray like this...

"Bless the Lord, O my soul; and all that is within me, bless Your holy name. Bless the Lord, O my soul, and I will never forget everything you have done for me. You have forgiven me of all my sins. I don't need to live in shame because I am forgiven. You have healed me from every disease. I don't ever have to be sick again. You saved me from destruction. Everything the enemy tried to use to kill me has failed. Every stupid decision I made in the past loses its power over me. You protect me. You cover me with lovingkindness and tender mercies. You are not like earthly people who change their opinion of me daily. You are always good. You have shown me mercy and will continue with mercy every day of my life. You satisfy my mouth with good things. Everything you have for me is good. When you correct me, it's good. When you direct me, it's good. What you provide for me is good. The spouse and children you have given me are good. I am satisfied with everything that has come from you. My youth is renewed like the eagles. I am not getting weaker as I grow older. I am getting stronger in my body and my spirit. My mind is sharper today than it was yesterday. I have more energy than people half my age because You renew my strength. Bless Your holy name!"

Whew—I got blessed just writing that prayer! Imagine the blessing if you take even 15 minutes every day to praise Him from His Word. The book of Psalms is filled with praise that you can make your own.

You can pray any of God's Word, but here's one more example. This is a prayer of petition—asking God for something. Ephesians 1 records a prayer Paul prayed for the church. I pray this almost every day for myself, my family, and my church.

> I have not stopped giving thanks for you, remembering you in my prayers. I keep asking that the God of our Lord Jesus Christ, the glorious Father, may give you the Spirit of wisdom and revelation so that you may know him better.
> I pray that the eyes of your heart may be enlightened in order that you may know the hope to which he has called you, the riches of his glorious inheritance in his holy people, and his incomparably great power for us who believe. That power is

> the same as the mighty strength he exerted
> when he raised Christ from the dead and
> seated him at his right hand in the
> heavenly realms, far above all rule and
> authority, power and dominion, and every
> name that is invoked, not only in the
> present age but also in the one to come.
>
> — EPHESIANS 1:16-21 NIV

Now make this Scripture your own prayer. Pray, "Father, give ME the Spirit of wisdom and revelation so that I may know You better." You get the picture. There are more prayers of Paul in Ephesians, Philippians, and Colossians. They are powerful, biblical prayers. They are not weak and self-centered. Pray the Word, and you will move from five-minute boring prayers to hours-long power prayers.

PRAY EARNEST AND HEARTFELT PRAYERS

Prayer is not a religious requirement. It is a passionate connection with your Father. If you're not feeling it, God's not hearing it. God hears people who worship and pray in Spirit and in Truth, according to John 4.

> Yet a time is coming and has now come when
> the true worshipers will worship the Father
> in the Spirit and in truth, for they are the
> kind of worshipers the Father seeks.
>
> — JOHN 4:23 NIV

God doesn't want you to recite nursery rhymes to Him. So, you start with thanksgiving and praise. It stirs you up in your spirit, so you pray with passion!

PRAY IN FAITH

Everything you receive from God, you receive by faith. Everything you do must be done in faith. Faith is the currency of God's Kingdom. Prayer is no different. Jesus told us…

> So Jesus answered and said to them, "Have faith in God. For assuredly, I say to you, whoever says to this mountain, 'Be removed and be cast into the sea,' and does not doubt in his heart, but believes that those things he says will be done, he will have whatever he says. Therefore I say to you, whatever things you ask when you pray, believe that you receive them, and you will have them."
>
> — MARK 11:22-24 NKJV

Believing often comes before receiving. This belief is faith. Once you have brought your request to God, thank Him that He hears you and is working on your behalf. Do not end prayer to start your day by saying things like, "Well, I prayed about it; we'll see if God heard me." Those are words of unbelief. Throughout the day, say, "Thank you, God, for hearing my prayer this morning. I know you've answered me."

PRAY IN THE SPIRIT

You learned how to be baptized with the Holy Spirit in chapter four. Once you are baptized in the Holy Spirit, you have a heavenly prayer language. You can pray in tongues (pray in the Spirit) at any time. Do it every day. It's not just for special occasions or revival meetings.

When you pray in the Spirit, the Holy Spirit prays through you. He prays precisely what is needed in every situation.

> So too the [Holy] Spirit comes to our aid and bears us up in our weakness; for we do not know what prayer to offer nor how to offer it worthily as we ought, but the Spirit Himself goes to meet our supplication and pleads in our behalf with unspeakable yearnings and groanings too deep for utterance.
>
> — ROMANS 8:26 AMPC

You have a way of praying that bypasses your mind. When you don't know what to pray for, the Holy Spirit helps you. But YOU must pray. He doesn't take you over and make you pray.

Praying in the Spirit builds you up in your inner man (your spirit man). When your inner man or spirit man is strong, your flesh falls in line behind him. So, praying in the Spirit brings your flesh into subjection to your reborn spirit man.

> But you, beloved, build yourselves up [founded] on your most holy faith [make

progress, rise like an edifice higher and higher], praying in the Holy Spirit;

— JUDE 1:20 AMPC

Do you want to grow spiritually? Pray in the Spirit every day!

ADDITIONAL RESOURCES

- *11 Things You'll Never Have Until You're Baptized in the Holy Spirit and Speak in Tongues* – Jonathan Shuttlesworth – Revival Today App
- *Prayer Secrets* by Kenneth E. Hagin

6

THE BIBLE

THE BIBLE IS IMPORTANT

The Word of God—the Bible—is your lifeline. The Word shows you who you are, who your Heavenly Father is, who Jesus is, what belongs to you now that you're a Christian, and how to live this life successfully.

You might be thinking, "I thought Jesus was my lifeline." Jesus is called the Word made flesh. He is the living Word of God. The Word is Jesus in print. Don't try to separate the two.

Read the Bible every day. Please don't read it as a religious requirement but as a daily meal through which you receive power for the day. You wouldn't go a whole day without giving your body food, and you shouldn't go an entire day without giving your spirit food. You don't get religious points for the number of chapters you read each day—you get something much more valuable. You get knowledge and power from the scriptures you read; understand, believe, and put them into practice!

The Bible is not just a good book. The Bible is the inspired Word of God. It is Truth. It contains no error. It is entirely reliable to guide your life. The Bible is God speaking to you today. Any teaching, tradition, popular opinion, or person—even your own thoughts—that speaks something contrary to what is contained in the Bible is a lie.

The Bible must be the supreme authority in your life—even when your opinion or experience differs from it. It's all or nothing. If you only accept part of the Word, you make yourself the ultimate authority in the places you do not receive. In essence, you are placing yourself higher than God. You are making yourself your own god. Therefore, you'll only get what you can provide for yourself.

The truth is...

> All Scripture is inspired by God and is useful to teach us what is true and to make us realize what is wrong in our lives. It corrects us when we are wrong and teaches us to do what is right. God uses it to prepare and equip his people to do every good work.
>
> — 2 TIMOTHY 3:16-17 NLT

God's Word is alive. It is not a dry, dead set of rules. It is a book of wisdom and instruction. When you search through the Word like you are in search of a great treasure, you find the path to an abundant life.

> For the word of God is living and powerful, and sharper than any two-edged sword,

> piercing even to the division of soul and spirit, and of joints and marrow, and is a discerner of the thoughts and intents of the heart.
>
> — HEBREWS 4:12 NKJV

God's Word is like a mirror. It shows you clearly—without any filter. As you read the Word, you see areas of your life where you are in disobedience. It shows you attitudes and actions you have in your life that God has forbidden. Then, you can repent and get in line with the Word. It's not just corrective; it's also instructive. The Word also shows you how to please God and walk in His blessings. The Word shows you how to succeed financially. The Word shows you how to have healthy relationships, be physically healthy, have peace and joy, and much more.

CHOOSING A BIBLE

In Mark 4, Jesus said that when people hear the Word (you hear it by reading it) and accept it, it produces something in their lives.

> "And the seed that fell on good soil represents those who hear and accept God's word and produce a harvest of thirty, sixty, or even a hundred times as much as had been planted!"
>
> — MARK 4:20 NLT

Choose a Bible you can understand. For new Christians, a version like the New Living Translation or New International Version is a great place to start. They are written in plain English. For example...

> If you openly declare that Jesus is Lord and believe in your heart that God raised him from the dead, you will be saved. For it is by believing in your heart that you are made right with God, and it is by openly declaring your faith that you are saved.
>
> — ROMANS 10:9-10 NLT

Many Bibles are available online, but you should have a physical Bible you can read. Some Bible apps enable you to compare verses in several translations. Choosing a Bible you can easily read and understand is the most important thing. Then, read it every day.

You can select a Bible containing just the scriptures or a study Bible like the Fire Bible by Life Publishers or Dake's Annotated Reference Bible. The Fire Bible contains study notes, commentary, articles, book introductions, and much more. The Dake's Bible is written in the King James Version; even if it is hard for you to understand King James, it is worth the price for the treasure trove of study notes included. As you get excited about the Word, you'll want to collect several translations and types of Bibles.

Once you choose your Bible, read and study it every day. Build a new habit of daily Bible reading. Start by reading one of the gospels (Matthew, Mark, Luke, or John), then read through the rest of the New Testament—Acts through

Revelation. These books are God's instructions to the church…you are the church.

Another helpful tool is The YouVersion Bible from Life Church. It offers many Bible translations in one place. It also has daily devotions from Spirit-filled teachers like Kenneth Copeland and Jerry Savelle. The Olive Tree Bible App is also good; it has commentary and much more. Both apps are free.

There is so much available today online and in print to help you understand God's Word. Get in the daily habit of spending time in the Word.

ADDITIONAL RESOURCES

- From Faith to Faith 365 Day Daily Devotional by Kenneth and Gloria Copeland on the YouVersion Bible App

7

CHURCH MATTERS

FINDING A CHURCH

Every born-again believer needs a church home. God sets you in a body of believers so you mature under strong teaching, have a support system of people who believe like you do, and have a place to serve. Choosing a good church will be one of God's greatest blessings. When you find a good church, it is a joy to go there and fulfill the command to meet together.

> ...not giving up meeting together, as some are in the habit of doing, but encouraging one another—and all the more as you see the Day approaching.
>
> — HEBREWS 10:25 NIV

As I write this, the COVID-19 panic is settling down. Millions of people quit attending church in person during the pandemic. Many of those people never came back to church. New Day Christian Center never quit meeting. As a result, the believers grew in numbers and strength. Make no mistake, as we draw nearer to Christ's return, more crazy things will happen. Scripture promises as much.

> He replied: "Watch out that you are not deceived. For many will come in my name, claiming, 'I am he,' and, 'The time is near.' Do not follow them. When you hear of wars and uprisings, do not be frightened. These things must happen first, but the end will not come right away." Then he said to them: "Nation will rise against nation, and kingdom against kingdom. There will be great earthquakes, famines and pestilences in various places, and fearful events and great signs from heaven. "But before all this, they will seize you and persecute you. They will hand you over to synagogues and put you in prison, and you will be brought before kings and governors, and all on account of my name. And so you will bear testimony to me. But make up your mind not to worry beforehand how you will defend yourselves. For I will give you words and wisdom that none of your adversaries will be able to resist or contradict. You will be betrayed even by parents, brothers and sisters, relatives and

> friends, and they will put some of you to
> death. Everyone will hate you because of
> me. But not a hair of your head will perish.
> Stand firm, and you will win life.
>
> — LUKE 21:8-19 NIV

None of these things to come are reasons to quit going to church—ever.

THE RIGHT CHURCH

Many people have traditional church homes with which their family has identified for generations. Yet, they never hear the gospel in a way that brings them to salvation. Don't go there! Do not be loyal to tradition; be loyal to Jesus.

The church where you were saved would be the obvious choice for you to attend if you can. This is where you heard the gospel in power and received Christ; that is the mark of a great church. If you cannot attend the church where you got saved, here are some "non-negotiables" for identifying a great church.

A SPIRIT-FILLED, HOLY SPIRIT HONORING CHURCH.

A Spirit-filled church believes, teaches, and promotes the baptism in the Holy Spirit with the evidence of speaking in tongues. The baptism of the Holy Spirit and the gifts of the Holy Spirit should be in operation in every area, from children's church to senior ministry. Tongues and supernatural demonstrations of God's power should be included in every service—not just during revivals. The authentic move of the Holy Spirit should be welcomed. Paul warns us...

> Do not stifle the Holy Spirit. Do not scoff at prophecies, but test everything that is said. Hold on to what is good. Stay away from every kind of evil.
>
> — 1 THESSALONIANS 5:19-22 NLT

Any church not allowing the supernatural move of the Holy Spirit through Spirit baptism and the gifts of the Spirit is disobeying Christ. Jesus said He would send another Helper like himself who would abide with you forever—the Spirit of truth. If you reject the Helper, you reject Jesus. It is no small thing. It is not a matter of personal choice to choose a non-Spirit-filled church over a Spirit-filled church. It is a conscious choice to "stifle" the move of God's Holy Spirit in your life.

A CHURCH THAT HONORS THE BIBLE AS THE ULTIMATE AUTHORITY

Culture changes. Traditions change. The Word of God remains the same—reliable, useful, and true. You must find a church that follows the Word.

> All Scripture is inspired by God and is useful to teach us what is true and to make us realize what is wrong in our lives. It

> corrects us when we are wrong and teaches us to do what is right. God uses it to prepare and equip his people to do every good work.
>
> — 2 TIMOTHY 3:16-17 NLT

A church honors the Bible when God's Word is at the center of every teaching. The Word is promoted—not self-help, social justice, or political agendas. Most churches have a Statement of Beliefs. The first doctrine should be The Infallible Word of God or something similar. If the foundation of belief is anything other than the Word, their beliefs and practices will change with the culture.

A SOUL-WINNING CHURCH

Churches exist for three reasons: to worship God, disciple believers, and win the lost. Find a church that makes soul-winning a priority. Jesus commands us to win souls.

> Then Jesus came to them and said, "All authority in heaven and on earth has been given to me. Therefore go and make disciples of all nations, baptizing them in the name of the Father and of the Son and of the Holy Spirit, and teaching them to obey everything I have commanded you. And surely I am with you always, to the very end of the age."
>
> — MATTHEW 28:18-20 NIV

The primary reason for the Baptism of the Holy Spirit is to win souls.

> "But you will receive power when the Holy Spirit comes on you; and you will be my witnesses in Jerusalem, and in all Judea and Samaria, and to the ends of the earth."
>
> — ACTS 1:8 NIV

You have access to the supernatural power of God for a purpose—to bring the lost to Jesus. A soul-winning church is joyful because the believers focus on helping others find Jesus—not on petty squabbles inside the church. Soul-winning unites believers around a common purpose.

GO TO CHURCH

Once you find your church, attend every service you can. Arrange your schedule around attending church. Don't make plans for Sundays or whatever midweek night the church meets. Don't sign your children up for sports that play on Sundays. Don't sleep in because it's your day off. Make church a priority.

Your pastors and teachers are gifts from God to help you mature in Christ. Your growth is directly related to church attendance; don't take it lightly.

Become a member of your church and serve there; be a blessing. Be open to whatever opportunity God gives you to minister. From being a greeter or a parking lot attendant to teaching, do something. As you serve, you mature and discover your gifts.

ADDITIONAL RESOURCES

- *The Soul Winning Script* from Revival Ministries International
- *The Assignment* by Dr. Mike Murdock

8

THE BODY AND BLOOD OF JESUS

THE BODY AND BLOOD SET YOU APART

The body and the blood of Jesus have delivered you from death and disease. To understand this, you need to go back to the book of Exodus. God's people—the Israelites—were slaves in Egypt. The time for their deliverance had come, so God raised Moses to lead them out of captivity. Moses told Pharaoh to let God's people go. Pharaoh refused, and a series of plagues were unleashed on the Egyptians. Pharaoh would not relent until the last plague, the killing of the firstborn.

The firstborn males of every family and all livestock in Egypt were to be killed. But God provided a way of protection and provision for His people. Each Israelite family was to do three things. First, they were to choose a perfect lamb from their flocks, sacrifice it, and sprinkle its blood on the doorposts of their houses. When the Lord came through to kill the firstborn, He would "pass over" the houses where He saw the blood on the doorpost. Second, they were to roast the body of the lamb and eat it inside their houses that night while dressed with their cloaks tucked in, shoes on, and staffs in their hands. Finally, they were to ask their Egyptian neighbors for silver, gold, and fine linens.

> So the people of Israel did just as the Lord had commanded through Moses and Aaron. And that night at midnight, the Lord struck down all the firstborn sons in the land of Egypt, from the firstborn son of Pharaoh, who sat on his throne, to the firstborn son of the prisoner in the dungeon. Even the firstborn of their livestock were killed. Pharaoh and all his officials and all the people of Egypt woke up during the night, and loud wailing was heard throughout the land of Egypt. There was not a single house where someone had not died. Pharaoh sent for Moses and Aaron during the night. "Get out!" he ordered. "Leave my people—and take the rest of the Israelites with you! Go and worship the Lord as you have requested. Take your flocks and herds, as you said, and be gone. Go, but bless me as you leave." All the Egyptians urged the people of Israel to get out of the land as quickly as possible, for they thought, "We will all die!" The Israelites took their bread dough before yeast was added. They wrapped their kneading boards in their cloaks and carried them on their shoulders. And the people of Israel did as Moses had

> instructed; they asked the Egyptians for clothing and articles of silver and gold. The Lord caused the Egyptians to look favorably on the Israelites, and they gave the Israelites whatever they asked for. So they stripped the Egyptians of their wealth!"
>
> — EXODUS 12:28-36 NLT

God made a distinction between Egypt and Israel that night. The Egyptians suffered the loss of their sons and possessions, while the Israelites saw God's protection and provision. They were preserved from death because of the lamb's blood on their doorposts. Not one Israelite died; they were delivered from captivity. 600,000 men plus women and children walked out of Egypt that night, and they were all healthy!

> He also brought them out with silver and gold,
>   And there was none feeble among His tribes.
>
> — PSALMS 105:37 NKJV

Think about a crowd that size—two million or more people. There must have been some elderly who couldn't walk, people with incurable diseases, babies born with birth defects, or those who had been beaten and abused in captivity. Yet, as they left, there was no feeble (sick or injured) person among them. Something extraordinary happened inside those houses that night. They were healed as they ate the body of the lamb. They had to eat the meal fully dressed because they were about to go somewhere. And, because they obeyed the word of the Lord to ask the Egyptians for their possessions, they left with the riches of Egypt!

The Lord told them they were to remember this night forever by observing the Feast of Unleavened Bread or the Passover meal each year. And they did. From the first Passover night in Egypt until the evening Jesus shared the Passover meal with his disciples, they ate and drank to remember the lamb's body and blood which had delivered God's people from captivity.

THE POWER OF THE BODY

When Jesus ate this meal with his disciples, they all understood what they were celebrating—God's deliverance through the lamb's body and blood. But Jesus flipped the script and showed them who the real Lamb was.

> ...and when He had given thanks, He broke it and said, "Take, eat; this is My body which is broken for you; do this in remembrance of Me."
>
> — I CORINTHIANS 11:24 NKJV

Jesus said, "this is MY body." It's not the lamb's body. It is Jesus' body. Jesus is the true Lamb of God. The Israelites had eaten the body of the lamb and received healing. Now, the body of the true Lamb would be given for our healing forever.

Isaiah prophesies about Jesus and the healing released from His beaten body...

> Surely He has borne our griefs (sicknesses, weaknesses, and distresses) and carried our sorrows and pains [of punishment], yet we [ignorantly] considered Him stricken, smitten, and afflicted by God [as if with leprosy]. But He was wounded for our transgressions, He was bruised for our guilt and iniquities; the chastisement [needful to obtain] peace and well-being for us was upon Him, and with the stripes [that wounded] Him we are healed and made whole.
>
> — ISAIAH 53:4-5 AMPC

Some say the healing spoken of in Isaiah is strictly a spiritual healing. But, the indisputable proof of Isaiah 53 pointing to physical healing is found in Matthew 8:16-17.

> That evening many demon-possessed people were brought to Jesus. He cast out the evil spirits with a simple command, and he healed all the sick. This fulfilled the word of the Lord through the prophet Isaiah, who said, "He took our sicknesses and removed our diseases."
>
> — MATTHEW 8:16-17 NLT

Praise God! The body of Jesus is for your physical healing. You are healed of every disease and affliction. You are delivered from every demonic oppression. You are healed from every mental and emotional sickness. You have healing forever because the body of Jesus was given to you! Healing was accomplished at the cross of Jesus. Nothing more is needed for you to be healed. To receive healing today, receive what the body of Jesus did for you. That is power!

THE POWER OF THE BLOOD

> In the same manner He also took the cup after supper, saying, "This cup is the new covenant in My blood. This do, as often as you drink it, in remembrance of Me."
>
> — I CORINTHIANS 11:25 NKJV

Jesus said, "this is MY blood"! It's not the lamb's blood. It is the blood of the true Lamb of God. The Israelites put blood on their doorposts and were saved from death. Now, the blood of the true Lamb is placed on the doorposts of our hearts, saving us from eternal death.

I covered this in the first chapter, but it's worth repeating. You are now saved from death because of the blood of Jesus. You have been transferred to a new kingdom—the kingdom of God's Son. Every sin is gone. You are made new. You are no longer under the curse of your old master, Satan. You are under Abraham's blessing, including the financial blessing the Israelites received when they left Egypt. You have the promise of eternal life because of the blood of the true Lamb, Jesus Christ!

It is easy to see what happened to the Israelites. Maybe it's not easy to believe these promises are for you today. I've got good news for you... The promises you have for today are even better than those the Israelites experienced because you are under a new covenant—a better covenant.

> But now Jesus, our High Priest, has been given a ministry that is far superior to the old priesthood, for he is the one who mediates for us a far better covenant with God, based on better promises.
>
> — HEBREWS 8:6 NLT

Jesus, the true Passover Lamb, is the One who brought you into a right relationship with your Heavenly Father and released you into what Peter calls "exceedingly great and precious promises."

> …by which have been given to us exceedingly great and precious promises, that through these you may be partakers of the divine nature, having escaped the corruption that is in the world through lust.
>
> — II PETER 1:4 NKJV

HOLY COMMUNION

Today, the Passover meal is called Holy Communion. The Israelites were commanded to observe the meal to remember their deliverance. Jesus commands all believers to observe Holy Communion to remember His sacrifice for deliverance from sickness and death.

When you eat the bread, you remember His body was beaten for your healing. When you drink the juice, you remember His blood sets you free from sin and death.

When you take communion, let it stir up your faith. As you eat the bread, thank God that you are healed by the stripes of Jesus. As you drink the juice, thank God that you are cleansed of all sin. Remember, the victory was accomplished at the cross. Nothing more needs to be done for you to be saved or healed. It is finished. Hallelujah!

ADDITIONAL RESOURCES

- *The Blood Covenant* by E.W. Kenyon
- *Healing the Sick* by T.L. Osborn

9

YOUR AUTHORITY

AUTHORITY DEFINED

Authority is delegated power. For the believer, authority is the power of Jesus delegated or given to you. Jesus gave you this power because He expects you to use it to walk in victory over the Devil and over anything the Devil tries to put on you. Yet, most Christians never grasp this concept. They often mistake poverty and powerlessness for humility and accept the things Jesus has overcome. This is not your story—you have something more!

Understanding authority is as easy as one, two, three—Ephesians one, two, and three. You must see where Christ is, where you are, and why.

WHERE CHRIST IS

Ephesians 1 declares that Christ is seated in the place of honor at His Father's right hand in Heaven.

> I also pray that you will understand the incredible greatness of God's power for us who believe him. This is the same mighty power that raised Christ from the dead and seated him in the place of honor at God's right hand in the heavenly realms. Now he is far above any ruler or authority or power or leader or anything else—not only in this world but also in the world to come. God has put all things under the authority of Christ and has made him head over all things for the benefit of the church. And the church is his body; it is made full and complete by Christ, who fills all things everywhere with himself.
>
> — EPHESIANS 1:19-23 NLT

Jesus Christ is above everything. He is above every ruler, every authority, every power, every leader, and everything else. He rules not only in this present world, but in the coming world, where there will be a new Heaven and a new Earth. There is no earthly ruler or government that outranks Him. There is no mightier power.

Jesus sits at the right hand of His Father, God. That is the seat of ultimate power and authority. Paul goes into more detail in Philippians.

> Therefore, God elevated him to the place of highest honor and gave him the name above all other names, that at the name of Jesus every knee should bow, in heaven

> and on earth and under the earth, and every
> tongue declare that Jesus Christ is Lord, to
> the glory of God the Father.
>
> — PHILIPPIANS 2:9-11 NLT

Jesus is King in three realms—in Heaven, on Earth, and under the Earth (demonic realm). He has the power to command all beings; every being will bow to Him and declare He is Lord. That's not some low-level power; that is universe-shaking power.

WHERE YOU ARE

Ephesians 2 declares that you are seated with Christ in the heavenly realms because you are united with Jesus.

> But God is so rich in mercy, and he loved us
> so much, that even though we were dead
> because of our sins, he gave us life when
> he raised Christ from the dead. (It is only
> by God's grace that you have been saved!)
> For he raised us from the dead along with
> Christ and seated us with him in the
> heavenly realms because we are united
> with Christ Jesus.
>
> — EPHESIANS 2:4-6 NLT

You cannot be saved unless you are united with Christ. So, every Christian is seated with Christ in heavenly places This is the seat of ultimate power and authority.

It's reasonable to believe Jesus has ultimate authority. You can believe Jesus can command demons to flee and sickness to go. But it's not as easy to believe He delegated the authority to you to do the same thing.

The proof of this truth is in Matthew 28. Jesus told his disciples He had been given all authority (after His death and resurrection). He took the authority back from Satan, who had it because Adam and Eve gave it to him in the garden when they sinned. As soon as Jesus got the authority back, He gave it to you so you could do God's work on Earth.

> Jesus came and told his disciples, "I have been given all authority in heaven and on earth. Therefore, go and make disciples of all the nations, baptizing them in the name of the Father and the Son and the Holy Spirit. Teach these new disciples to obey all the commands I have given you. And be sure of this: I am with you always, even to the end of the age."
>
> — MATTHEW 28:18-20 NLT

> "Look, I have given you authority over all the power of the enemy, and you can walk among snakes and scorpions and crush them. Nothing will injure you."
>
> — LUKE 10:19 NLT

> For in Christ lives all the fullness of God in a

> human body. So you also are complete
> through your union with Christ, who is the
> head over every ruler and authority.
>
> — COLOSSIANS 2:9-10 NLT

You are seated with Christ in heavenly places. You have been delegated the power of Jesus Christ. You have the authority of Christ!

WHY

In Ephesians 3, the "why" is revealed. God did all this to show the demonic powers His great wisdom through the church.

> God's purpose in all this was to use the church
> to display his wisdom in its rich variety to
> all the unseen rulers and authorities in the
> heavenly places. This was his eternal plan,
> which he carried out through Christ Jesus
> our Lord.
>
> — EPHESIANS 3:10-11 NLT

Simply put, your life is to demonstrate to the Devil and his demons that Christ won the victory over them.

According to Ephesians 1, Jesus is the head of the church for your benefit, and the church is His body. Jesus gives the decrees and orders as the head; you carry them out as the body. So, the power you are given through Jesus is to carry out His will on this earth. His will is to deliver all whom the Devil oppresses.

> And you know that God anointed Jesus of Nazareth with the Holy Spirit and with power. Then Jesus went around doing good and healing all who were oppressed by the devil, for God was with him.
>
> — ACTS OF THE APOSTLES 10:38 NLT

The purpose of the authority you have been given is to do the same things Jesus did.

> "I tell you the truth, anyone who believes in me will do the same works I have done, and even greater works, because I am going to be with the Father."
>
> — JOHN 14:12 NLT

> "Go and announce to them that the Kingdom of Heaven is near. Heal the sick, raise the dead, cure those with leprosy, and cast out demons. Give as freely as you have received!"
>
> — MATTHEW 10:7-8 NLT

You command demons in His Name when you understand the authority Jesus has given you. You lay hands on the sick and command the sickness to go. You use this authority in your own life to set others free. What you cannot do is claim you are powerless. Your life constantly reminds the Devil that he has lost it all in Jesus' name.

ADDITIONAL RESOURCES

- *The Believer's Authority* by Kenneth E. Hagin

10

GIVING

TITHES AND OFFERINGS

Money is a big part of your life. No matter what some religious people say, life is better when you have enough money. Ask the single mother working two jobs who can't take her child to the doctor if money is important. Money is the currency of this world. It is what we use to do business. Money is neither good nor evil. It is neutral. It is the love of money that causes destruction.

> For the love of money is the root of all kinds
> of evil. And some people, craving money,
> have wandered from the true faith and
> pierced themselves with many sorrows.
>
> —1 TIMOTHY 6:10 NLT

It is possible to have great wealth and not love money more than God. The Old Testament men of God like Abraham, Isaac, Jacob, Joseph, David, and Solomon all had great wealth. In fact, their wealth was a reward from God for their faithfulness and obedience. Money did not come between any of these men and their love of God.

It is the same for you today. God desires for you to prosper. He also desires for you to keep money in its proper place in your heart. So, God has instituted a system of giving that will ensure both. This is the giving of the tithes and offerings.

From Abraham to Moses, to the prophet Malachi, to Jesus, to the writer of Hebrews, the command to give both the tithe and offering is reinforced for every believer. We are promised a curse if we disobey and a blessing if we obey.

> "Should people cheat God? Yet you have cheated me!"
> "But you ask, 'What do you mean? When did we ever cheat you?'
> "You have cheated me of the tithes and offerings due to me. You are under a curse, for your whole nation has been cheating me. Bring all the tithes into the storehouse so there will be enough food in my Temple. If you do," says the Lord of Heaven's Armies, "I will open the windows of heaven for you. I will pour out a blessing so great you won't have enough room to take it in! Try it! Put me to the test!"
>
> — MALACHI 3:8-10 NLT

The word "tithe" means a tenth or ten percent. So, every believer is required to give ten percent of everything that comes into his hand. If your salary is $1,000 a week, your tithe is $100 a week. An offering is what you decide to give. You may give another $50 or $100 or even more as an offering. In Malachi, God promises He will open the windows of Heaven and pour out a blessing so big you won't have room for it all. Then you'll want to give more That's a system you want to be part of!

SEEDTIME AND HARVEST

Another principle in play here is seedtime and harvest. When you plant a seed, you get a harvest. Money is a seed you plant into God's kingdom and He promises the harvest in proportion to what you plant.

> Remember this: Whoever sows sparingly will also reap sparingly, and whoever sows generously will also reap generously. Each of you should give what you have decided in your heart to give, not reluctantly or under compulsion, for God loves a cheerful giver. And God is able to bless you abundantly, so that in all things at all times, having all that you need, you will abound in every good work. As it is written: "They have freely scattered their gifts to the poor; their righteousness endures forever." Now he who supplies seed to the sower and bread for food will also supply and increase your store of seed and will enlarge the harvest of your righteousness. You will be enriched in every way so that you can be generous on

> every occasion, and through us your
> generosity will result in thanksgiving
> to God.
>
> — 2 CORINTHIANS 9:6-11 NIV

God owns everything on Earth and in Heaven. There is no one wealthier than He is. Yet, He chooses for wealth to pass through the hands of His people to fund everything for His Kingdom. It takes money to spread the gospel. If you give, God's work happens quickly and efficiently, and you are blessed in return. If you do not give, God's work is delayed and difficult, and you miss the blessing.

> "Give, and it will be given to you. A good
> measure, pressed down, shaken together
> and running over, will be poured into your
> lap. For with the measure you use, it will
> be measured to you."
>
> — LUKE 6:38 NIV

Be a tither and a giver from day one. Get into God's system of financial blessing and you will never lack anything in your life!

ADDITIONAL RESOURCES

- *Financial Overflow* by Jonathan Shuttlesworth

PART III

KEEP MOVING UPWARD

11

YOU DON'T HAVE TO SIN

SIN SEPARATES

Sinning keeps you from moving upward in your Christian life. If you don't decisively deal with sin, it inevitably causes you to turn away from Jesus and lose your salvation. That's the bad news. The good news is that you don't have to sin. God has given you everything you need to live a life that is pleasing to Him. It is possible to live a holy life through the power of the Holy Spirit.

Every born-again believer knows not to sin. The problem is that you may not know you don't have to sin. The religious people in Jesus' day told people not to sin, but they didn't offer them any help. Jesus is different. He came as a man, demonstrated a life without sin, defeated sin, then gave you everything you need to overcome sin.

My youngest son, Ben, preached a powerful sermon to our church when he was just 16 years old. I'll never forget one thing he said, "Nobody gets taken out because Satan is so strong. We get taken out because we don't understand what God has given us." This is completely true. It's scriptural.

> "my people are destroyed from lack of knowledge…"
>
> — HOSEA 4:6 NIV

Jesus said…

> "And you shall know the truth, and the truth shall make you free."
>
> — JOHN 8:32 NKJV

Only the truth you know sets you free. People are sick today because they don't understand that Jesus has delivered them —healed of every sickness. People are depressed today because they don't understand that the joy of the Lord is their strength. People are in bondage to sin because they don't understand that Jesus has given them everything they need to live above sin. Defeated people don't have a power problem; they have an understanding problem.

POWER OVER SIN

It's not even a fair fight. You have tremendous power over Satan and sin. Jesus has already defeated Satan. You're not here to win the battle again. You're here to walk in the victory won by Jesus. When Jesus won, He did it right. He disarmed and humiliated Satan through the cross.

> And having disarmed the powers and
> authorities, he made a public spectacle of
> them, triumphing over them by the cross.
>
> — COLOSSIANS 2:15 NIV

Your enemy is disarmed, and you are armed with the spiritual nuclear weapon, the Holy Spirit.

> You are of God, little children, and have
> overcome them, because He who is in you
> is greater than he who is in the world.
>
> — I JOHN 4:4 NKJV

When Paul prays for the church in Ephesus (Ephesians 1:15-23), he prays they would understand the greatness of the power God has made available to them. He doesn't pray they will never face difficulties or have an easy life. He knew it was inevitable that trials and temptation would come. He prayed they would understand they have power from the Holy Spirit to overcome anything that tries to harass them. You have this same power!

> Ever since I first heard of your strong faith in
> the Lord Jesus and your love for God's
> people everywhere, I have not stopped
> thanking God for you. I pray for you
> constantly, asking God, the glorious Father
> of our Lord Jesus Christ, to give you
> spiritual wisdom and insight so that you
> might grow in your knowledge of God. I
> pray that your hearts will be flooded with

> light so that you can understand the confident hope he has given to those he called—his holy people who are his rich and glorious inheritance. I also pray that you will understand the incredible greatness of God's power for us who believe him. This is the same mighty power that raised Christ from the dead and seated him in the place of honor at God's right hand in the heavenly realms. Now he is far above any ruler or authority or power or leader or anything else—not only in this world but also in the world to come. God has put all things under the authority of Christ and has made him head over all things for the benefit of the church. And the church is his body; it is made full and complete by Christ, who fills all things everywhere with himself.
>
> — EPHESIANS 1:15-23 NLT

Now that you are saved and baptized in the Holy Spirit, God's power living inside you gives you the ability to say NO to every temptation to sin. Don't look at yourself as a helpless sinner. You are a child of God. The same Spirit who raised Jesus from the dead is living inside of you. Satan will try to tempt you, but you don't have to fall for it.

TEMPTATION IS PREDICTABLE, TEMPORARY, AND NOT FROM GOD

> When tempted, no one should say, "God is tempting me." For God cannot be tempted by evil, nor does he tempt anyone; but each person is tempted when they are dragged away by their own evil desire and enticed. Then, after desire has conceived, it gives birth to sin; and sin, when it is full-grown, gives birth to death.
>
> — JAMES 1:13-15 NIV

Don't get confused. Temptation isn't from God. He's not playing with you. Your Father wants you to succeed. You do, however, have an enemy, Satan. He will tempt you. You also have a carnal nature (your flesh) that desires ungodly things. Your flesh must be crucified or denied. Your "spirit within" is born-again—new. You must strengthen your spirit through the Word and praying in the Spirit.

There is a predictable progression to sin. You are enticed (tempted). When temptation is not dealt with, you sin. When sin is not dealt with, you die. But God has provided a way out.

You can stop temptation while it is still a desire. This is what Jesus did; this is why He never sinned. A desire is nothing more than a thought. Every action starts as a thought. You have the power to control your thoughts; that's what spiritual warfare is.

> For though we walk in the flesh, we do not war according to the flesh. For the weapons of our warfare are not carnal but mighty in God for pulling down strongholds, casting down arguments and every high thing that exalts itself against the knowledge of God, bringing every thought into captivity to the obedience of Christ,
>
> — II CORINTHIANS 10:3-5 NKJV

This is what Jesus did in the wilderness when Satan tempted him. Satan came to plant thoughts or desires in Jesus' mind. Jesus took "every thought into captivity to the obedience of Christ." He stopped the thought; He didn't dwell on it. Then, He spoke the Word of God to counteract the thought.

> Then Jesus was led by the Spirit into the wilderness to be tempted by the devil. After fasting forty days and forty nights, he was hungry. The tempter came to him and said, "If you are the Son of God, tell these stones to become bread." Jesus answered, "It is written: 'Man shall not live on bread alone, but on every word that comes from the mouth of God.'" Then the devil took him to the holy city and had him stand on the highest point of the temple. "If you are the Son of God," he said, "throw yourself down. For it is written: " 'He will command his angels concerning you, and they will lift you up in their

> hands, so that you will not strike your foot against a stone.'" Jesus answered him, "It is also written: 'Do not put the Lord your God to the test.'" Again, the devil took him to a very high mountain and showed him all the kingdoms of the world and their splendor. "All this I will give you," he said, "if you will bow down and worship me." Jesus said to him, "Away from me, Satan! For it is written: 'Worship the Lord your God, and serve him only.'" Then the devil left him, and angels came and attended him.
>
> — MATTHEW 4:1-11 NIV

Here's how this plays out in your life. When you are tempted to look at something you shouldn't—like pornography or a movie you shouldn't watch—realize temptation is not from God. He's not testing you to see if you're strong enough. The temptation to sin comes from either your enemy or your own flesh. Take the thought captive and bring it into obedience to Christ. Stop the thought; don't dwell on it. Then find something in the Word of God to counteract it. In this example, Proverbs 4:23 is a powerful weapon.

> Guard your heart above all else, for it determines the course of your life.
>
> — PROVERBS 4:23 NLT

You say, "I will not look at this thing because the Word says I must guard my heart above all else. What I let into my heart through my eyes and ears will determine the course of my life. If I look at this thing, it won't be long before I'm tempted to do this thing. I'm stopping this right here and now."

You don't have to act on temptation!

Temptation is temporary. Temptation comes for a moment; it will not last forever. There is a way out. Use the Word like Jesus did and pray. Pray this, "Father, my flesh wants to do this thing but, I know you've given me power over it. I am trusting you and I will not give in. Thank you for power in Jesus' name!" Pray in the Spirit. This type of prayer bypasses your mind (desires) to give you victory.

> Submit yourselves, then, to God. Resist the devil, and he will flee from you. Come near to God and he will come near to you. Wash your hands, you sinners, and purify your hearts, you double-minded.
>
> — JAMES 4:7-8 NIV

When you resist the Devil, he flees from you. He left Jesus in the desert when he saw he wasn't getting anywhere with him. He'll leave you when he sees you know how to use your spiritual weapons. He'll return again, but you'll be ready for him every time.

What happens if you don't stop temptation when it's just a desire? You sin. Temptation is not a sin. That's why it is so important to stop it there. Sin happens when you commit the act you were thinking about. If you sin, you must repent.

> If we confess our sins, he is faithful and just
> and will forgive us our sins and purify us
> from all unrighteousness.
>
> — 1 JOHN 1:9 NIV

Quickly ask your Heavenly Father to forgive you. Don't hide or justify your sin. Confess it and keep moving forward. Learn from it. Eliminate things and places from your life if they are a constant temptation. Don't go to places where you are tempted to sin. Get rid of your smartphone if you are tempted to look at things you shouldn't. Sin is not a small thing; we must take it seriously.

> "So if your eye—even your good eye—causes
> you to lust, gouge it out and throw it away.
> It is better for you to lose one part of your
> body than for your whole body to be
> thrown into hell. And if your hand—even
> your stronger hand—causes you to sin, cut
> it off and throw it away. It is better for you
> to lose one part of your body than for your
> whole body to be thrown into hell."
>
> — MATTHEW 5:29-30 NLT

Jesus knew the seriousness of sin. He knew the damage sin causes. You must take sin seriously too. If there are people, places, or things causing great temptation to sin, avoid them.

When sin is repeated again and again, it becomes a stronghold. You become a slave to it.

> Don't you know that when you offer
> yourselves to someone as obedient slaves,
> you are slaves of the one you obey—
> whether you are slaves to sin, which leads
> to death, or to obedience, which leads to
> righteousness?
>
> — ROMANS 6:16 NIV

Sin leads to your death as a child of God. You can lose your salvation when you repeatedly give yourself to sin. Find a strong, Christian friend who holds you accountable. Ask them to check on you regularly. Be honest with them and ask for their help. Talk to your pastor or a church leader. You don't have to be destroyed by sin; you won't be you if you learn to deal with every temptation. God has given you a way out!

> The temptations in your life are no different
> from what others experience. And God is
> faithful. He will not allow the temptation
> to be more than you can stand. When you
> are tempted, he will show you a way out so
> that you can endure.
>
> — 1 CORINTHIANS 10:13 NLT

SIN IS A CHEAP COUNTERFEIT

God is the creator of every good thing. Satan has nothing good to offer you; he takes the good things of God and counterfeits them hoping to deceive you. Every sin you are tempted with is a cheap counterfeit of something better that God offers you. Alcohol is a great example.

> Don't be drunk with wine, because that will
> ruin your life. Instead, be filled with the
> Holy Spirit...
>
> — EPHESIANS 5:18 NLT

Being drunk is a cheap imitation of being filled with the Holy Spirit. Yet, a significant number of Christians settle for this counterfeit every weekend. Drunkenness causes you to make stupid decisions and do things you regret. I know many ministers who thought they could mess around with alcohol. Today, none of them are in ministry because they did something stupid, like having an affair or getting a DUI.

There is something so much better. Be filled with the Spirit of God! The Holy Spirit will give you joy and peace. When you are filled with the Spirit, you do things that lead to a great life and great relationships. Don't fall for imitations.

> For the kingdom of God is not a matter of
> eating and drinking, but of righteousness,
> peace and joy in the Holy Spirit...
>
> — ROMANS 14:17 NIV

> Don't be deceived, my dear brothers and
> sisters. Every good and perfect gift is from
> above, coming down from the Father of
> the heavenly lights, who does not change
> like shifting shadows.
>
> — JAMES 1:16-17 NIV

God has good things in store for you. I pray that you experience the fullness of everything He has for you. Don't miss out. You do not have to sin!

ADDITIONAL RESOURCES

- *The Battlefield of the Mind* by Joyce Meyer
- *Drawing Near* by John Bevere

12

NEVER STOP

FIRED UP

You are on a path that leads you upward in life. Never stop growing and increasing. Continue to grow in your relationship with the Lord by studying His Word, praying passionately, and sitting under anointed preachers and teachers. Especially pay attention to the Word of God.

> We must pay the most careful attention,
> therefore, to what we have heard, so that
> we do not drift away.
>
> — HEBREWS 2:1 NIV

Whether you've been a Christian for one week or many decades, you need the Word of God to keep you from drifting back to your old ways of thinking and living. Never stop devouring the Word.

Don't listen to old friends or even family members who tell you to calm down about your new life. Stay fired up about the things of God. He is taking you somewhere. Surround yourself with people who encourage you to grow in your faith.

I pray this book is a helpful companion to you as you sit under godly pastors and teachers. I pray you find a group of friends who encourage you to serve God with all your heart. You don't have to do this alone. You have a family now!

> Therefore, since we are surrounded by such a great cloud of witnesses, let us throw off everything that hinders and the sin that so easily entangles. And let us run with perseverance the race marked out for us…
>
> — HEBREWS 12:1 NIV

You are surrounded by a cloud of witnesses like Moses, Abraham, Noah, Samson, Rahab, and many others. They are cheering you on from Heaven telling you to "strip off every weight that slows you down, especially the sin that so easily trips you up" and to "run with endurance the race God has set before you."

These great men and women of faith who have lived and died serving God, are looking down from Heaven to cheer you on. They're telling you, "It's worth it! Don't ever give up!"

The best is yet to come when you keep serving the Lord. Don't ever stop!

GOD LOVES YOU AND HAS A GREAT PLAN FOR YOUR LIFE.

IT STARTS WITH SALVATION

- **Romans 3:23** - Everyone has sinned; we all fall short of God's glorious standard.
- **Romans 6:23** - The wages (cost) of sin is death, but the free gift of God is eternal life through Christ Jesus our Lord.
- **Romans 5:8** - But God showed his great love for us by sending Christ to die for us while we were still sinners.
- **Romans 10:9** - If you declare with your mouth, "Jesus is Lord," and believe in your heart that God raised him from the dead, you will be saved.

You can pray something like this:

> Father, I know I've sinned, and I'm sorry for my sin. I ask you to forgive me. I believe your Son, Jesus, died for my sin and you raised Him from the dead so I could be declared forgiven. I confess you as my Savior and Lord. Thank you for saving me.
>
> In Jesus' name. Amen

DON'T DELAY ONE MORE DAY

God loves you so much that He sent His Son to die for YOU. (John 3:16)

Very soon, Jesus will come back for every person who has received Him as their Savior. (2 Peter 3:9-10)

Be saved today!

ABOUT THE AUTHOR

Angel Adams is the pastor of New Day Christian Center in Wellsburg, WV. She is dedicated to preaching the gospel and activating Christians to walk in the power and authority of Jesus Christ. Angel and her husband, Scott, have reached generations of children, youth, and adults in the Ohio Valley with the gospel message for over 20 years.

- facebook.com/angel.adams.355
- instagram.com/angeladams20
- youtube.com/@newdaychristiancenter3492

CPSIA information can be obtained
at www.ICGtesting.com
Printed in the USA
JSHW020424300123
36992JS00004B/26

9 781644 576069